# Fresh, Canned, and Frozen
## *Food from Past to Future*

By William Wise     Illustrated by Shelley Fink

*Parents' Magazine Press · New York*

A Stepping-Stone Book

# Contents

# 1. Food Today

Food is important to us for two reasons. When we eat the right food, it helps us to stay in good health. And when we eat food that we like, it gives us pleasure.

A great deal of food is grown in the world today. And yet people often go hungry. Sometimes they do not have money to buy the food they need.

In some countries, people have enough food but do not get much pleasure from it. They may not have refrigeration to keep their food from spoiling. Or they may live where there are no trucks or trains to bring them food from other places. So they have only a few foods to choose from.

Today in America we have enough refrigeration to keep our food from spoiling. We also have many foods to choose from. When we go shopping, if we have the money to spend, we can buy almost any kind of food we like.

For many of us who live in the cities of America and Europe, food is easy to get now. We are able to buy foods that are fresh, frozen, or canned. Trucks and trains often bring different foods to us from hundreds of miles away.

If we want to, we can do all our shopping in

one store—a supermarket. Or we can shop in stores that "specialize." We can buy meat in a butcher shop, and bread and cake in a bakery. We can buy fruit and vegetables in a special fruit and vegetable market.

Many Americans do not even have to go to a store to get their food. They can place an order by telephone. Later, the store will deliver the food to the customer's home.

But all of this is very new. Until just a few years ago, most people in the world found it hard to get food they liked. And far too often, they could not get enough food, and so they went hungry.

# 2. *Man, the Hunter*

Thousands of years ago, it was not easy for primitive people to get their food. When we speak of these early people now, we call them primitive, which means first. A number of primitive families usually joined together to form a tribe. They made their home in caves. Each tribe had to get all of its own food, for it lived too far away from other people to share or trade.

To get food for their families, men spent most of their lives hunting wild animals. Sometimes they dug a deep pit and covered it with grass. When an animal fell into the pit, they killed it with heavy stones. If the animal was large enough, everyone had a feast.

The first people did not know how to make fire. So they never cooked their food. When they killed an animal, they ate it raw.

If hunting was poor, people ate smaller

animals that were easier to catch. They ate
lizards, rabbits, and snakes. They also ate fish and
birds. The children may have helped by learning
to catch fish with their hands. They may have
learned to kill birds by hitting them with stones.

Primitive people added to their diet by
gathering nuts in the forests. During the summer
and fall they collected wild fruit from trees,

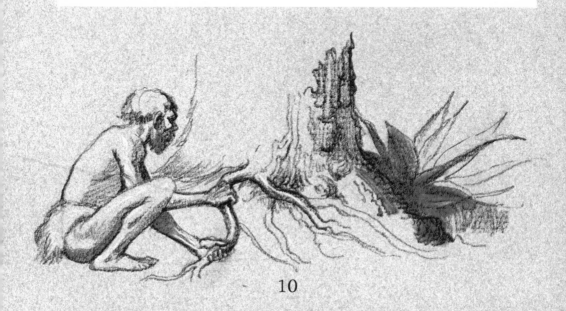

bushes, and vines. They dug up roots.
They picked wild vegetables and
grasses. If they lived near the sea,
they ate clams and snails. They also
ate insects. These people thought a
few grasshoppers, or a handful of
beetles, made a tasty dish.

As the years passed, men learned
new skills. They learned how to make
fish hooks out of animal bones. By
using a hook on the end of a line,
they could catch more fish. They
also learned how to make spears,
and bows and arrows.

In time, people discovered how to make fire.
Sometimes they rubbed two pieces of wood
together, and caught the sparks in dry leaves
or grass. Sometimes they hit two pieces of flint
together, and caught the sparks. After that they
could warm themselves with a fire in their caves.

One day, another discovery was made. Maybe a
grass fire burned some animals, and a hunter
found them. To his surprise, the animals smelled
good. He started to eat one of them. The roasted
meat was soft and easy to chew. It tasted better
than raw meat. Later he told others about his
discovery, and from then on, cave fires were
used for cooking.

Primitive families now had a warm home, and a new way of preparing meat, fish, and birds. But they still did not eat very well. When they kept their food too long, it spoiled. And when hunting was bad there wasn't enough food, so everyone went hungry.

## 3. Animals and Seeds

It took men thousands of years to change from hunting to farming. The first step came when they caught a number of wild animals. In the north, they caught reindeer. In other parts of the world, they caught pigs, horses, cows, sheep, and goats.

Little by little, people learned how to tame these animals. They learned how to feed them, and how to keep them safe from harm. Raising tame, or domestic animals, was a better way of getting

meat than hunting for it. And from their reindeer, goats, and cows, people also found they could get other foods, like butter, milk, and cheese.

Cheese-making was probably discovered by accident. Somehow, people learned that milk could be turned into a different food by placing it inside an animal-skin bag and shaking it. After a while, the milk would separate into two parts. There would be the watery part, called the

"whey," and the lumpy, cheese-like part, called the "curd." In many countries, people discovered that this lumpy "cheese" was a delicious new food.

As time went by, primitive people also learned that the seeds of certain grasses were good to eat. Just as important, they saw that if the seeds fell to the ground, some of them soon sprouted into new plants.

But why leave the growing to chance? Why not pick some of the seeds from the stalks, put them into the ground, and raise all the new seeds that were wanted?

In different parts of the world, people learned

how to grow wheat, barley, corn, and other kinds of grain. When the harvest was ready, the stalks were cut down. Then the seeds were shaken out, and crushed between two stones to make a rough kind of flour. After water had been added, the flour was shaped into flat cakes and placed on hot stones. The heat baked the cakes into a heavy, dark sort of bread.

People also learned how to make clay pottery. This was a useful discovery. Grain could be ground into flour in a deep pot, and less would be wasted. Food could be stored in pots and jars. Water, too, could be kept in jars and carried

from place to place. After that, people no longer had to live by the edge of a river or lake in order to have water.

Slowly life grew a little easier. Men spent less time hunting. Instead, they raised domestic animals, grain, vegetables, and fruit. Some families moved to towns and cities.
They had a better supply of food, so they began to think of new ways to prepare it. Soon they were enjoying their meals as never before.

Even so, the fight against hunger was far from over. There was more food now, but there were more people to eat it, and no way had yet been found to keep many foods from spoiling. Also, there were risks in farming that no one understood at first.

Man, the Hunter, often had starved. As the years went by, Man, the Farmer, learned that sometimes he still faced the same danger.

# 4. Locust, Drought, and Flood

Rain was very important to the early farmer.
When there was enough, his crops grew tall and
he had a fine harvest. But when the rains failed to
come, causing a drought, the crops turned brown
and died.

A bad drought meant there would be little
bread, fruit, or vegetables in a country.
Sometimes, too, farmers had no grass
to feed their domestic animals. So they killed

and ate their own pigs, cows, and sheep, before the animals died of starvation. After that, nobody had meat, milk, or cheese to eat. It was a time of famine, and many people went hungry.

There were other ways that a country's crops could fail. In some years, just as the wheat or barley was growing tall, a swarm of locusts darkened the sky. Before long, the ground was covered by millions of these insects.

Each locust in the swarm could eat its own weight in a single day. The locusts ate everything green—the fields of grain, the leaves of the trees, the smallest blades of grass. In a few

hours the entire harvest was lost, and famine
soon followed.

Farmers had other troubles, too. Disease
often killed their grain. Wind or hail blew down
their crops. Mice and rats ate the food they grew.
Sometimes, instead of drought, there was too
much rain, and the rivers flooded the fields. A
season of flooding usually meant a year of
famine.

In some countries, the land itself gave out.
The more times a field was planted, the poorer the
crops seemed to become. Early farmers did not
understand that all living things need food. The

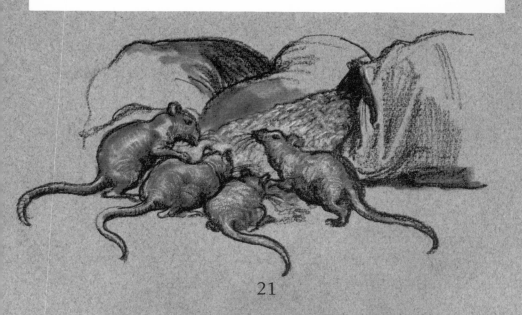

crops they grew each year took plant food—
minerals like potash and phosphate—out of the
soil. After a few years, so little plant food was
left in the soil that a good crop could no longer
be raised.

Then the farmers cut down more trees, and
planted new fields. The old land was left to
itself. Sometimes it turned into a desert, where
not even wild grass could grow.

# 5. "Worth Its Weight in Gold"

People have often gone hungry because they could not grow enough food. They have gone hungry, too, because their food "turned bad," or spoiled, before they could eat it.

Men have tried different ways of keeping food from spoiling. In early times, meat, fish, and certain fruits were preserved by drying them in the sun. This kept them good to eat for many days. Or a piece of meat was placed

over a smoky fire. The smoke "cured" the meat, so that weeks later it could still be eaten.

Another way to keep food from spoiling was to store it in a cool place. People kept food in caves and cellars. In Rome, a few rich families built ice houses, where they could store foods that spoiled quickly.

One of the best ways to preserve meat and fish was to salt them. But this was not always possible. Today, we can go to a store and buy a box of salt for a few cents. For thousands of years, however, salt was scarce and expensive. Most of it came from mines deep in the earth. Or it was made from sea water. In some countries, salt was so hard to get that it was said to be "worth its weight in gold."

People also used salt as a flavoring, to make their food taste better. Roman soldiers were so fond of putting salt on their food that they were given a little each day as part of their wages. The salt they received was called "salarium." Our own word for pay—"salary"—comes from this old Latin word.

After a long time, the cities of Europe grew larger. Some men became rich. Those with money to spend were eager to buy things from distant countries. They wanted sugar for cakes and candy. And they wanted spices to season their food.

Pepper was one of their favorite spices. It added a pleasant flavor to many dishes. And when

the dishes began to spoil, nothing hid the bad taste better than pepper.

But pepper, like salt, was very expensive. The small pepper seeds came from the Far East —from India and the Spice Islands. Only the Arabs knew this, and they kept the secret to themselves. For many years, Arabs rode their camels back and forth across the hot desert sands. Arab traders grew rich, buying pepper in the East, and selling it in the West.

At last, people in Europe learned where spices grew. To get them, men built wooden ships and went on long, dangerous voyages. In 1492, when Christopher Columbus sailed from Spain, he hoped to reach the Spice Islands. Instead, he discovered America. Five years later, in 1497, Vasco de Gama, a Portuguese captain, sailed to India and returned with a cargo of spices. From then on, pepper, cloves, nutmeg, and cinnamon were brought back to Europe by sea. As the years went by spices became cheaper, so that more people could use them to flavor their food and make it taste better.

# 6. Turkeys and Indians

On their travels, sea captains like Christopher
Columbus discovered many new foods.
In North and South America, they tasted
tomatoes, turkeys, potatoes, Indian corn, and
chocolate for the first time. On their return,
they took these foods back to Europe.

New foods moved in the other direction too.
There were no chickens, cows, or pigs in America
until the first settlers brought a few from

Europe. The settlers also brought wheat and apple seeds to plant in the new land.

The settlers could not bring all the food they needed, though. Their ships were very small. And the ocean trip took so long that some of their supplies turned bad and couldn't be eaten. So, when they reached America, they had to start gathering food at once.

The early settlers in New England, who were called Pilgrims, got most of their meat by hunting. The forests were filled with birds and other animals. Children helped their families by hunting the smaller animals, and by catching fish in nearby rivers and lakes.

Many of the settlers knew hardly anything about raising crops. To make things worse, they had come to a strange country, where the soil and weather were different from at home. They asked the Indians for advice. The Indians were able to help them because they had lived in America for many years and knew about the soil and the weather.

The Indians taught the Pilgrims how to grow corn and beans. They showed them the way to mix corn and beans together to make succotash, a dish we still enjoy. The Indians also showed them how to make corn bread, and how to draw the sweet sap from maple trees, to make into syrup and a delicious brown sugar.

In October, 1621, the Pilgrims held the first Thanksgiving in America. They invited Chief Massasoit and ninety of his Indian tribe to join in the three-day celebration.

The Indians brought five deer to the feast. The Pilgrims gave their guests many good things to eat, too. They shared geese, ducks, shrimp, and lobster. They also ate wheat and corn bread, salad greens, plums, and berries. And they had one other food that everyone always thinks of on Thanksgiving day—they had plenty of turkey.

The turkeys that we eat today, though, are not wild birds. Our turkeys are domestic birds, raised on turkey farms.

It took farmers many years to learn how to raise domestic turkeys. For a while, no matter what the farmers did, most of the birds would not eat, and so they starved to death.

Finally, a scientist found out the reason. For

a few days after hatching, young turkeys are almost blind. When they put down their heads to eat, they cannot see the food on the ground. The scientist learned that baby turkeys can see their food when it is colored bright green and placed on a shelf, a foot or so off the ground.

Because they know this now, American farmers have much less trouble raising domestic turkeys. And each year at Thanksgiving, millions of us can buy, cook, and enjoy our favorite holiday bird.

# 7. The Food Spoilers

A hundred years ago, most American families still lived on small farms. They grew more food than they needed themselves. To earn money, they sold the rest of their crops to people who lived in nearby towns and cities.

From spring until fall, a few cows gave the farmer milk, butter, and cheese. By late fall, though, there was hardly any food left for the bigger domestic animals. Then the farmer killed some of his cattle and pigs, and salted them for the winter. Whenever he had chickens or other meat to spare, the farmer put them on a wagon, drove into town, and sold them. He also sold milk, butter, eggs, and cheese whenever he could.

Often a farm family dug a tunnel into a hillside, and used it as a root cellar. In this cool, dark place, they kept apples, potatoes, cabbages, and turnips. They had no refrigerators, but sometimes they built an ice house by a shallow pond. When the pond froze in the winter, the

farmer and his sons cut out blocks of ice. They stored the blocks in the ice house. Then their butter and milk would keep fresh until it could be sold or eaten.

If there was no pond on his land, the farmer sometimes built a small stone house near a spring. Cold water from the spring could be made to run through the spring house, cooling the air inside.

In cities and towns, people did not have refrigerators, either. But some families did own a wooden icebox. They bought blocks of ice from an ice company. By using their icebox, they could keep food fresh for a day or two, until they were ready to eat it.

Although people had learned that they could, for a short time, prevent food from spoiling by keeping it cold, no one really understood why food turned bad. Then scientists discovered some of the reasons.

Now we know that air itself can harm certain foods. Nuts and butter, for instance, will spoil if they are left too long in the air. Bread, cake, and cookies will become stale, if they are not wrapped up and stored away. Oxygen, a gas that is in the air around us, brings these changes about. To stop this from happening, we must keep butter, nuts, and bakery products out of the open air.

We know that foods also can be spoiled by tiny plants called micro-organisms. Three kinds of micro-organisms are very harmful to foods. They are bacteria, yeasts, and molds. Bacteria are the smallest. These plants are so tiny that thousands can live on a speck of food. The only way to see bacteria is under a microscope.

Single yeast cells also are very small. They, too, can only be seen under a microscope.

A patch of mold, however, can be seen quite easily. You may have found some blue or green mold on a piece of bread. Or you may have found mold growing on a piece of fruit, or inside a jar of jam. Such food no longer is good to eat. Like any food that has spoiled, it should always be thrown away.

Scientists have learned how to keep certain micro-organisms from spoiling the things we eat. One way is to cook food at a high temperature and then seal it in an air-tight

bottle or can. Another way is to dry out food, so that no water is left in it. As long as food stays completely dry, micro-organisms will not be able to grow there. And when foods are stored under refrigeration, the micro-organisms either cannot grow at all, or grow so slowly that they do us no harm. Thanks to what scientists have learned, much of our food now stays good to eat for a long time.

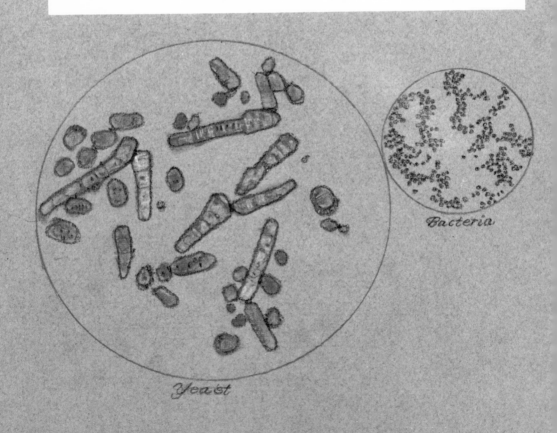

Bacteria

Yeast

# 8. Fresh, Canned, and Frozen

Many changes began to take place in America a hundred years ago. Farms became bigger. Farmers bought new machines and fertilizers, so they could grow larger crops. Some farmers started to "specialize"—to grow only fruit, vegetables, grain, or domestic animals. This helped them to raise more of one kind of food. Better roads were built, making it easier to move food from the farms to the cities. Many railroads also were

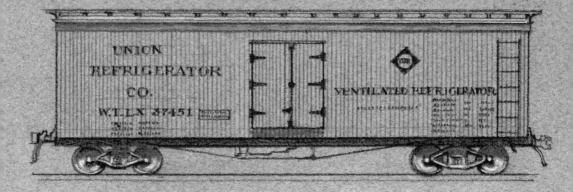

built. By using railroad cars, large amounts of food could be sent from one part of the country to another.

In the winter, some fresh foods could travel by train without being harmed. In the summer, though, meat, fish, and dairy products spoiled very quickly in the heat. Fruit and vegetables spoiled, too. So a way had to be found to keep fresh foods cool. The first refrigerator car was built about 1870. It had special tanks in which ice was stored. The ice kept the car cool for a while, even on a hot summer day.

Since then, we have learned a great deal about refrigeration. We now use new and better refrigerator cars for shipping food. We also use thousands of refrigerator trucks.

Some of our fresh foods travel for hundreds of miles. Oranges, for instance, come from Florida and California. Much of our lettuce is grown in Arizona. Apples come from all over the United States—from places as far apart as New York and Oregon. Bananas are shipped from Central America on refrigerator ships. Seventy million bunches of bananas every year come to the United States this way.

Many fruits and vegetables are picked before they are ripe. They are graded for quality by government inspectors of the U. S. Department of Agriculture. Then they are packed in boxes, plastic bags, and other containers, and shipped by truck and train to a cold storage warehouse. While being shipped and stored they are allowed to ripen under refrigeration, until they reach full flavor.

Our stores and homes also have refrigeration. So, at every point along the way, from farm to kitchen, many of our foods are kept cool, and do not spoil. Because of refrigeration, we enjoy fresh fruit, vegetables, meat, fish, and dairy products all year long.

Today, we also eat many kinds of canned foods. The first canning factory in America was very small. A few workers sealed the cans by hand. Sometimes the foods were good to eat. But sometimes when the cans were opened, the food inside had spoiled.

After scientists had learned about micro-organisms, it became possible to keep harmful bacteria, yeasts, and molds out of preserved foods. Now we have many large canning factories and other food-processing plants in the United States. Each day they prepare hundreds of different foods in clean, airless containers. Much of the work is done by machines. Weeks later, when we open a can of fruit juice or a bottle of ketchup, we know that the food inside will taste the way it did on the day it was prepared.

Preservatives, however, are sometimes added to these prepared foods to make them last even

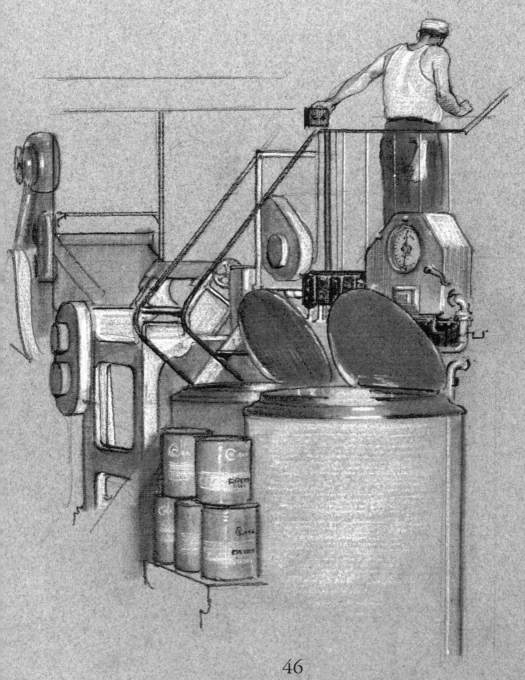

longer. These preservatives must be chosen with care. For some of them might make us sick, if we ate too much of them.

One of the newest ways of preserving food is to quick-freeze it. A few years ago, the first factories were built to quick-freeze fruits and vegetables. Before long, many "ready-to-eat" lunch and supper dishes also began to be cooked and frozen. Now cakes, pies, orange juice, and all sorts of other foods are frozen, packaged, and sold. Frozen foods often make it easier for us to prepare our meals. And they add to our eating pleasure by giving us more dishes to choose from.

# 9. America's Favorites

In the past fifty or a hundred years, many families from other parts of the world have come to live in America. Often they brought different foods with them from the countries they left behind—foods that all Americans have learned to enjoy.

Hamburgers were first eaten in America by settlers who came here from Hamburg, in Germany. They cooked and seasoned the meat and ate it that way. Then, in 1904, a man at the St. Louis World's Fair thought of selling a hamburger inside a bun. Hamburgers quickly became an American favorite. Today, Americans eat millions of hamburgers a week.

"Hot dogs," or frankfurters, are another of our favorite foods. The first "franks" were made almost a hundred years ago, and also came to us from Germany—from Frankfurt. Like hamburgers, they were sold without a bun. To keep customers from burning their fingers, a pair of white cotton gloves was given away free, with each "red hot."

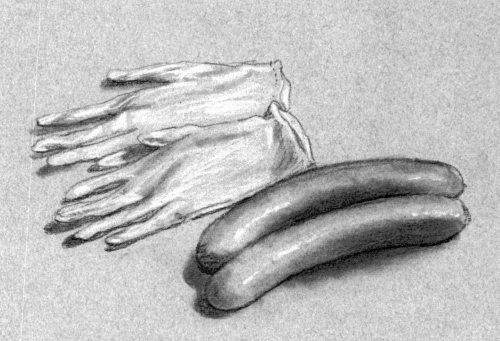

After a bun was added, the hot dog became very popular. Americans now eat fifteen *billion* hot dogs every year!

The pizza is one of our newest favorites. The word "pizza" means pie in Italian. Different kinds of pizzas have been made in Italy for many years. When American soldiers were in Italy during the Second World War, a number of them tasted a pizza for the first time. They liked the Italian pie. After the war they came back to America and told others about it. Soon, small stores sprang up all over the country—stores where you could buy a hot pizza to eat right there, or to take home. Now we can even buy frozen pizzas in some of our food stores.

Nobody knows where ice cream was made first. Some people think it was invented in Italy. We do know that four hundred years ago, an Italian princess went to France to marry the French king. She took along her own cooks, who taught the French how to make "iced cream."

A hundred years later, the King of England served ice cream to his guests at a dinner party. In another hundred years, ice cream was being eaten in America. The first American to own an ice cream freezer was George Washington. He

spent two hundred dollars in one year, to have ice cream in his home.

Since 1900, ice cream has been America's favorite dessert. Today, we eat more ice cream than any other country. We eat three billion quarts each year, and enjoy every delicious spoonful!

There is hardly any country in the world that has not given us at least one food to enjoy. Many Americans like to eat French bread, sometimes with a rich French cheese. Italian bread is popular, too.

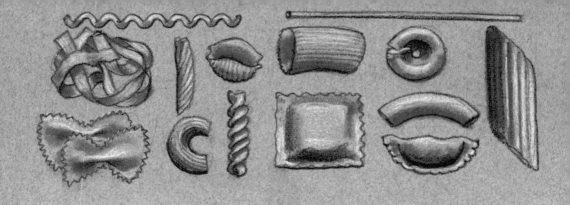

Spaghetti and macaroni came to us from Italy. Mexico gave us tortillas—thin pancakes of corn, baked on an iron or stove. Hungary gave us goulash, a kind of stew. People from Holland taught us to eat cole slaw, and Won Ton soup was brought to us from distant China. Some of us like borscht, a Russian soup that is made from beets.

A number of our most popular foods, though, were invented in America. One of them was first made less than a hundred years ago. A doctor in the South wanted to cure some sick children. He

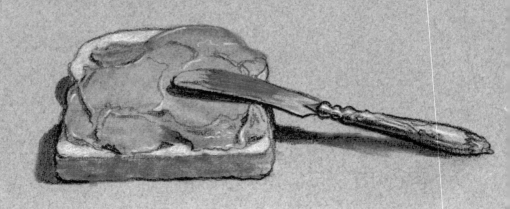

thought a different diet might help them to get well. So, he took some peanuts and mashed them up. The children enjoyed the doctor's "peanut butter." It wasn't long before peanut butter was being sold and eaten by Americans everywhere.

Many of America's "Southern" dishes were first made by black people from Africa. They were such good cooks that in time these dishes—especially "Southern fried chicken"—were enjoyed all over America.

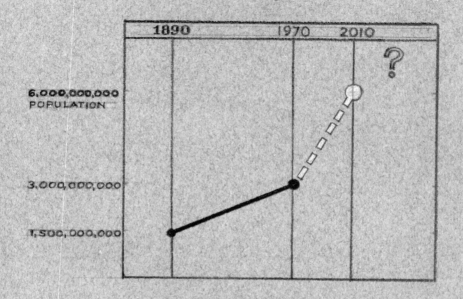

# 10. Our Numbers Grow

Today in America, we have many different foods. We know how to keep them from spoiling. We know how to ship them all over the country, and all around the world. We have learned a great deal about food—and yet, we have not learned how to keep people from going hungry.

The number of people in the world has doubled in the last eighty years. Soon, our numbers will double again. There are more than three billion of

us now. In about forty years, *six or seven billion* people may be living on our planet!

Farmers and scientists have worked hard to raise more food for our growing population. To do so, they have had to learn more about domestic animals, plant disease, seeds, and soil.

Farmers today know how to make better use of their land. When they want to return plant food to the soil, they use animal manure, or other natural or artificial fertilizers.

In certain places, farmers have learned that they should not always grow the same crop. After raising wheat, they may grow clover or alfalfa. This kind of farming is called "crop rotation."

Machinery is being used on many farms. Giant tractors, reapers, and threshers, for instance, help a smaller number of men to grow more food.

Farmers now have better ways to get water to their fields. In many countries, huge dams have been built. When drought comes, these dams

provide the farmers with water. And when there has been too much rain, the dams hold back the rivers and keep them from flooding the land.

Plant disease still troubles today's farmer. Scientists have not been able to find a complete cure for the two worst diseases, the "rusts" and the "smuts."

The rusts and the smuts are fungus diseases. The rusts may be the worst enemy of the wheat

grower. But the smut diseases are bad enough. Each year, they spoil two percent of the world's grain—enough to make ten billion loaves of bread!

Scientists also have helped American farmers to raise better domestic animals. Our cows give richer milk now. Pigs and steers give more meat. Chickens grow fatter, and lay more eggs.

Farmers in other countries are being helped, too. Scientists have developed a new kind of rice. Eastern countries like Japan, India, China, and Indonesia need rice as we need wheat. The new "wonder" rice may give these countries much bigger harvests.

Each year, though, there are more people in the world, so each year we need more food. In some countries today, there are millions of hungry people. When their crops fail, famine comes, and many of them starve. So the fight against hunger still goes on—as it has for thousands of years—and the fight has yet to be won.

# 11. Food for Tomorrow

Because there soon will be so many more of us in the world, we must add to our food supplies in any way that we can. New land will have to be planted. Still better use of the soil will be needed. Insects and plant disease must be made less harmful. Better farm machinery and fertilizers will lead to even larger harvests. And more people must have refrigeration to keep their food from spoiling.

Perhaps the sea can be made to give us more food. In Japan, men already have begun to "farm" the ocean. They now raise a vegetable-like seaweed, as other farmers grow vegetables on land. And some Japanese are trying to raise shrimps in seaside "farms."

Scientists are studying the ocean. They are trying to learn how more fish and other sea food can be caught or grown. They are studying tiny animals called plankton, that live in the sea. Perhaps one day plankton will be "farmed," and added to our food supply.

We cannot overlook anything, in our fight against hunger. By the year 2010, six or seven billion people will need enough food to keep in good health.

A great deal of work must be done before that. If it *is* done in time, the people of tomorrow will have enough to eat, as people seldom have, since primitive tribes first left their caves to hunt for food.

# Index